LOUISIANA

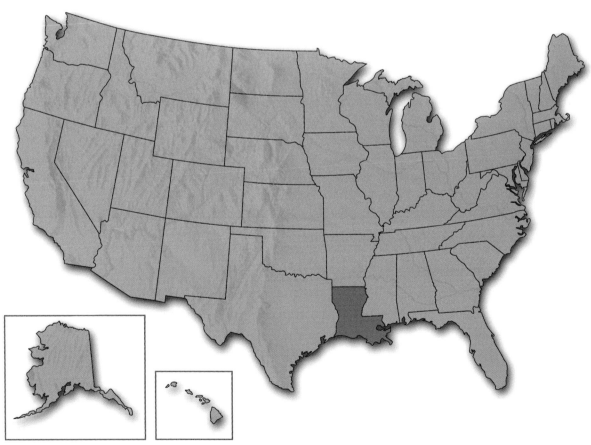

Robb Johnstone

Published by Weigl Publishers Inc.
123 South Broad Street, Box 227
Mankato, MN   56002
USA
Copyright © 2001 WEIGL PUBLISHERS INC.

Library of Congress Cataloging-in-Publication Data available upon request from the publisher. Fax: (507)388-2746 for the attention of the Publishing Records Department.

ISBN 1-930954-55-7

Printed in the United States of America
1 2 3 4 5 6 7 8 9 0   05 04 03 02 01

Editor
Rennay Craats
Design
Warren Clark
Copy Editor
Heather Kissock
Cover Design
Terry Paulhus
Layout
Derek Heck

Photograph Credits

Every reasonable effort has been made to trace ownership and to obtain permission to reprint copyright material. The publishers would be pleased to have any errors or omissions brought to their attention so that they may be corrected in subsequent printings.

Cover: Riverboat (Louisiana Office of Tourism), Crawfish (Lafayette Convention and Visitors Commission); **Mark Adkins:** page 22; **Archive Photos:** page 17, 19; **Chitimacha Tribe of Florida:** page 3, 16; **Corbis Corporation:** page 27; **Corel Corporation:** pages 3, 9, 10, 11, 13, 14, 15, 16, 19, 28, 29; **Digital Vision Corporation:** pages 9, 15; **Eyewire Corporation:** page 13; **Glenbow Archives, Calgary, Canada:** page 18 (NA-3232-45),18 (NA-1135-31), 18 (NA-1391-1); **Lafayette Convention and Visitors Commission:** pages 3, 6 (Danny Izzo),10 (Oscar Chandler), 12, 23 (Kent Hutslar), 24, 25, 28, 29; **Louisiana Office of Tourism:** pages 4, 5, 6, 8, 9, 10, 11, 12, 13, 16, 17, 20, 21, 24, 25, 26; **New Orleans Public Library:** pages 3, 7, 8, 15, 21, 24, 26, 27, 29; **New York Public Library:** page 6; **Photo Disc Corporation:** pages 3, 27; **Planetware:** pages 7, 21; **Visuals Unlimited:** pages 15, 19.

CONTENTS

INTRODUCTION

"Let the good times roll" is something you may hear shouted along the streets of New Orleans during **Mardi Gras** season in Louisiana. Of course, you may also hear "laissez les bon temps rouller," which means the same thing, but in French.

Louisiana is one of the most interesting and unique states in America. Its history is influenced by a French culture that still exists today. Its land is shaped by the mightiest river in North America, the Mississippi. Its people are a mix of cultures that come together every year for the biggest party in the country, Mardi Gras.

QUICK FACTS

The state capital of Louisiana is Baton Rouge.

Louisiana's nickname is the Pelican State. because pelicans are constant residents of the state. The state bird is the Eastern brown pelican.

The magnolia is Louisiana's state flower. Many people tried to make the iris the state flower and the magnolia the state tree. The bid was unsuccessful. Mississippi also has the magnolia as its state flower.

Louisiana's state tree is the bald cypress. It grows in many of the swampy areas.

The name "Mardi Gras" is French for "Fat Tuesday." This festival was named after the custom of leading a fat ox through the streets of Paris on Shrove Tuesday.

The Mississippi river is one of the busiest waterways in the world.

Getting There

Louisiana shares its borders with Arkansas, Mississippi, and Texas. The state's location where the Mississippi River empties into the Gulf of Mexico makes it one of the busiest commercial areas in the country.

Getting to Louisiana is as easy as following the Mississippi River south, or by driving south along Route 61, which starts at the Canadian border. Both routes cut through the center of the United States and end up in the colorful southern **port** city of New Orleans.

QUICK FACTS

The state songs are "Give Me Louisiana" and "You Are My Sunshine."

Louisiana entered the Union on April 30, 1812. It was the eighteenth state.

The state insect is the honeybee.

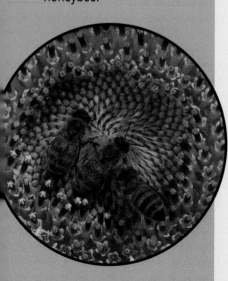

Location Map

GULF OF MEXICO

Louisiana has produced many celebrated artists, writers, musicians, and actors. Some of these celebrities include **jazz** musician Louis Armstrong, writer Truman Capote, musician Fats Domino, actress Dorothy Lamour, and singer Jerry Lee Lewis, just to name a few.

Good food is important to Louisianians and is a large part of their culture. In fact, some of the state's biggest celebrities are chefs, such as Paul Prudhomme and Emeril Legasse.

Gumbo takes its name from a Bantu word for okra, one of the dish's main ingredients.

When Louis Armstrong was young, he played trumpet in marching bands and on the Mississippi riverboats.

QUICK FACTS

Louisiana's state gem is the agate.

The state was named in honor of France's King Louis XIV in 1682.

The state flag is blue with a white and gold pelican found on the state seal in the center. Beneath is a white ribbon with the state motto, "Union, Justice, and Confidence," written on it.

Louisiana's history is filled with interesting characters, from priests and pirates to plantation owners and **voodoo** queens. Louisiana has a wide variety of people and cultures blending together in harmony. It is much like the popular Louisiana dish **gumbo**: no formal recipe, a rich combination of ingredients, and spicy and exotic flavors with every bite.

Marie Laveau, a legendary voodoo queen, was feared throughout nineteenth-century Louisiana.

QUICK FACTS

The Battle of New Orleans made future president Andrew Jackson a hero. The War of 1812, for which it was fought, ended two weeks earlier. It took more than a month before the news of the war's end reached Louisiana!

Milk is the official drink of Louisiana.

The state musical instrument is the accordion. It is used to play Cajun music.

Louisiana has a colorful history, with a mix of cultures and languages. Over history, the state has been governed under ten different flags.

LAND AND CLIMATE

Louisiana is known for its swamps and marshes. Its highest point, Driskill Mountain, is only 535 feet high. New Orleans, the lowest point in the state, is five feet below sea level. More than 7,400 square miles of Louisiana are under water. The low, wet land is excellent for raising crops, but it is also responsible for many floods. This is why long, high mounds called **levees** are built throughout the state to keep flood water from destroying homes and farmlands.

Louisiana is known for its **bayous**, which are small, slow-moving rivers. Bayous may branch off many times as they wander through the wetlands along the coast. Some bayous contain fresh water while others are brackish, which means they contain a combination of fresh water and salt water.

Louisiana's climate is humid in most areas, with mild winters and hot summers. The average January temperature in the south is 55° F, rising to an average of 82° F in July. Louisiana is also one of the wettest states. Rainfall averages 56 inches a year. Hurricanes swept in from the Gulf of Mexico sometimes hit Louisiana.

QUICK FACTS

Louisiana ranks thirty-first in size among American states.

If you include its many marshes, Louisiana has a coastline of 15,000 miles.

New Orleans is the wettest major city in the United States.

Some bayous contain fresh water and others contain a combination of fresh and salt water.

The record high temperature was 114° F on August 10, 1936. The lowest temperature ever in Louisiana was 27° F on February 13, 1899.

Hurricane Audrey killed 500 people in Louisiana in 1957. It was one of the state's worst disasters.

Overflowing bayous help enrich Louisiana's soil by leaving rich alluvium deposits.

NATURAL RESOURCES

Before the discovery of oil in Louisiana, agriculture and trapping were very important to the economy. Such crops as sugarcane and cotton were **vital**.

When oil was discovered in 1901, the Louisiana economy changed forever. Louisiana contains almost 10 percent of all known U.S. oil reserves. Its reserves of natural gas are even larger, with more than 25 percent of the nation's supply. Louisiana also has huge salt resources, contained in large underground formations. Some of these are a mile across and almost 50,000 feet deep. **Sulphur** is another important mineral. The first sulphur mined in America came from Louisiana.

With nearly 14 million acres of forests, Louisiana is also a major producer of lumber. Pine, oak, gum, and cypress trees are all harvested in the state.

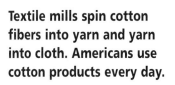

Textile mills spin cotton fibers into yarn and yarn into cloth. Americans use cotton products every day.

The lumber industry attracted large corporations to Louisiana during the late 1800s.

PLANTS AND ANIMALS

The wetlands of Louisiana are a natural haven for plants and animals. Here, there are plants, such as sedge grass, rushes, and palmetto scrub, that thrive on the wet conditions. Spanish moss hangs from the branches of cypress and oak trees, creating an eerie feeling in the swamps and marshes where they grow.

The thousands of ponds and bayous are home to bullfrogs, catfish, bass, and crayfish, which are called crawfish in Louisiana. American alligators, which are the state reptiles, are also now common in this area, despite being scarce in the last century. They live in the waters and lowlands of Louisiana and other southern states.

Alligators hiss at potential enemies as a warning sign.

The American white pelican is not afraid of travel. It migrates in the fall as far as Mexico and Central America.

The bird that gives Louisiana its nickname as the Pelican State is the brown pelican. It is becoming a rare sight. Its cousin, the white pelican, is much more common. Its nesting grounds are in the coastal marshes.

Wildlife abounds in Louisiana's swamps and marshes. Deer, wildcats, beavers, muskrats, otters, and raccoons can all be found in these areas.

Forests cover approximately half of the state. These areas are home to animals including rabbits, skunks, opossums, and gray foxes.

Otters are great swimmers and can stay underwater for as long as four minutes.

TOURISM

Louisiana celebrates the annual Mardi Gras festival that marks the end of the carnival season. The season begins on January 6 and lasts until around Easter. Parades begin the week before Mardi Gras, and residents and tourists alike celebrate in masks and fancy clothing. This event draws tourists from around the world.

Many visitors also come to Louisiana to taste its world famous cuisine. No trip is complete without sampling the flavors of Cajun and Creole dishes.

The plantation mansions are another popular tourist attraction. As plantation owners became wealthier, their homes became more elaborate. They tried to make life in the new world as graceful and elegant as possible. Many mansions are surrounded by large gardens with long, tree-lined avenues leading to the homes.

QUICK FACTS

Tourists spend an average of $5.2 billion in Louisiana every year.

Cajun is a combination of French and Southern cuisines. Cajun dishes include **jambalaya** and coush-coush, a thick cornmeal breakfast dish.

Creole is a combination of French, Spanish, and African cuisines. One of the most famous dishes of Creole heritage is gumbo.

The plantation culture came into being along the state's rivers and bayous, where planters first used the rich soil for **indigo** and tobacco. These crops were soon replaced by cotton in the north and sugarcane in the south.

In 1850, two-thirds of America's millionaires were plantation owners.

INDUSTRY

The invention of the steam engine was a blessing to Louisiana. Steam-powered riverboats traveled the Mississippi River, transporting goods and people. By 1840, New Orleans was the second-largest port in the country. Today, New Orleans is still an important port city. The largest industrial employer in the state is a shipyard in New Orleans. Here, vessels are sometimes built upside down and launched into the river sideways rather than the usual method of stern-first.

Oil refining is another major industry in Louisiana. It is estimated that the state's petroleum refineries produce enough gasoline each year to fill 800 million automobile gas tanks.

The fishing industry produces a lot of the nation's seafood. It is the largest producer of shrimp and oysters in the United States, and its catch includes crab, shrimp, red snapper, and tuna.

To catch crabs, fishers use pots that float beneath buoys near the water's surface.

The first important use of refined oil was a product called kerosene. It was used in oil-burning lamps.

QUICK FACTS

One oil refinery in Louisiana is the fourth largest in the Western Hemisphere.

Louisiana is the nation's largest handler of grain for export around the world.

The state's fishing industry catches about 25 percent of all the seafood in America.

Louisiana produces 60 million wooden matches a day, half of the nation's entire production.

America's only port capable of handling superships, the Superport, is located in Louisiana.

Besides gasoline, Louisiana refineries also produce jet fuels and 600 other petroleum products.

GOODS AND SERVICES

While much of Louisiana's economy depends on its natural resources, there are also many different goods and services that contribute to the overall picture. Louisiana manufactures hundreds of products, including telephone systems, light trucks, electrical equipment, glass products, automobile batteries, mobile homes, playground equipment, and clothing. It is also known for producing transportation equipment. Ships, truck trailers, and aircraft are important manufacturing products.

QUICK FACTS

Louisiana is among the top five states in the production of sugarcane, sweet potatoes, rice, and cotton.

Louisiana produces more furs than any other state.

Children have Louisiana to thank for many of the playgrounds they spend time on.

Louisiana is also important to the space program, providing vital goods and services. Fuel tanks for NASA's space shuttle program are built in New Orleans. NASA also operates an aerospace computer service center in Slidell.

Food processing is also important to Louisiana's economy. Its leading foods are coffee, sugar, and soft drinks. Beans brought in from Latin America are processed in a plant in New Orleans. Most of the state's major cities have soft-drink bottling factories. Sugar refineries are also prominent in Louisiana.

Space travel helps humans see Earth in relation to the entire universe.

FIRST NATIONS

Most of what we know today about Louisiana's Native culture is based on the records of European explorers who began arriving in the early 1600s. They encountered the Tunica, Muskhogeans, Chaddo, Attakapa, and Chitimacha. These groups all spoke different languages and had different cultures.

The Native peoples of Louisiana grew many different crops, including corn, pumpkins, squash, melons, and beans. They also gathered wild nuts and fruits, hunted game with blowguns and arrows, and set woven nets across streams to catch fish.

The encounter with Europeans was often disastrous for Native Americans. Although the Europeans had the advantage of firearms, the most dangerous weapon they carried with them was disease. The Native peoples had no **immunity** to these European illnesses. Many were wiped out after being exposed to diseases such as smallpox, measles, and tuberculosis.

QUICK FACTS

There is evidence to show that native civilization existed in Louisiana 3,000 years ago, in a place now called Poverty Point. That culture disappeared by about 700 BCE.

When Europeans arrived, around 12,000 Native peoples from thirty tribes lived in Louisiana.

The Chitimacha Tribe settled around the bayous of what is now southern Louisiana.

EXPLORERS

The King of Spain arranged for Europe's first organized exploration of Louisiana. He had heard stories of a river in the New World that was a rich source of gold. With this wealth in mind, he sent explorer Hernando De Soto to find the river.

In 1541, De Soto reached the Mississippi River. He and his men followed the river south, but De Soto died before they reached the mouth of the river. Still, his men were likely the first Europeans to set foot on Louisiana soil.

After giving up on becoming a priest, the adventurous René-Robert Cavelier, also called La Salle, arrived in Canada from France. In 1682, he set out by canoe down the Mississippi with a group of fellow explorers.

When the group arrived at the mouth of the Mississippi after a dangerous journey, La Salle put up a post with the French coat of arms and declared that the land belonged to the King of France, Louis XIV. Pierre Le Moyne founded a French settlement in what became Ocean Springs in 1699. This was the capital of the state until 1702.

Louis XIV chose the sun as his royal emblem and was called the Sun King.

Louisiana got its name from La Salle. The land was claimed for King Louis XIV, so the area was called Louisiana.

MISSIONARIES

During the years that Louisiana was a colony of France and Spain, Roman Catholic missionaries were a common sight in the territory. One reason is that there was a royal policy which stated that only Catholics could live in the colonies.

The kings of France and Spain paid priests and bishops to travel to Louisiana. The job of these missionaries was to bring Christianity to the Native Americans and to set up churches in the "New World." One group of Roman Catholics that did a lot of missionary work was the **Jesuit** order. The Jesuits brought European religion to the Native peoples and to slaves. They were very successful, especially with the African Americans.

By 1800, twice as many African Americans as whites were being baptized in the St. Louis Cathedral in New Orleans. Even though they took up the Christian faith, many African Americans continued to practice their African religions in secret.

Jesuits were founded by Saint Ignatius of Loyola in 1543. The name "Jesuit" stands for the Society of Jesus.

QUICK FACTS

Today, the mixture of Catholic and traditional African beliefs still exists in Louisiana.

Jesuits are members of a Roman Catholic religious order for men. The order was founded by Ignatius of Loyola in 1534.

EARLY SETTLERS

King Louis XIV knew he would have to defend his new territory against the British. He sent Pierre Le Moyne, also known as Iberville, to the mouth of the Mississippi to build a colony. Iberville arrived in 1699 and established a base at Biloxi Bay.

Pierre's brother, Jean Baptiste Le Moyne, was asked to set up a colony by a company wanting to build a trading center on the Mississippi River. In 1718, Le Moyne, also called Bienville, chose a spot south of Lake Ponchartrain and named the town *Nouvelle Orleans.* This means New Orleans in English.

In the early 1800s, the United States needed new territory to develop the western frontier. President Thomas Jefferson decided New Orleans and the Mississippi River system should belong to the United States. He sent American representatives to France to meet with Emperor Napoleon. After negotiations and the stroke of a pen, the residents of Louisiana went from being French to American in the deal that became known as the Louisiana Purchase.

QUICK FACTS

The Louisiana Purchase of 1803 was one of the best real estate bargains in history. For only $15 million, the United States acquired nearly one million square miles of land, doubling the size of the country.

Biloxi became the first capital of the new Louisiana colony.

New Orleans was named in honor of the Duc D'Orleans.

Napoleon did not want to sell Louisiana, but he needed money to pay for his wars in Europe.

American president Thomas Jefferson is best known as the man who wrote the Declaration of Independence.

POPULATION

The people of Louisiana are a mix of races and cultures. In 1996, whites made up 67 percent of the state's population and African Americans made up 31 percent. In comparison, the national average has whites making up 80 percent of the population and African Americans just 12 percent.

Nearly 70 percent of Louisiana's population lives in urban areas, such as the major cities of New Orleans and Baton Rouge. The remaining 30 percent live throughout the state in rural areas, such as towns, villages, and on farms.

QUICK FACTS

The largest city in Louisiana is New Orleans, with a population of approximately 477,000.

The second largest city is Baton Rouge, with about 216,000 people, followed by Shreveport with 192,000.

The population of the entire state is approximately 4.4 million people, according to a 1997 estimate.

Fishing is a wonderful pastime in rural Louisiana.

POLITICS AND GOVERNMENT

When Louisiana entered the Union in 1812, it brought with it a system of law that came from France. The system still exists today, while every other state in the nation follows the English common law system. The main difference between the two types of law is that judges in Louisiana rely on a system of written laws, while judges in other states are bound by the decisions made in earlier cases.

Another leftover from the days of French and Spanish rule is the political division of the state. Rather than counties, Louisiana is divided into sixty-four **parishes**, which were once managed by the Catholic Church. Today, most parishes are governed by a body called the police jury. No other state has this parish system.

QUICK FACTS

The capital of Louisiana is Baton Rouge, which means 'red stick' in French. It was named by an early explorer who spotted a red stick on a hill.

Louisiana has the tallest State Capitol in the country. The building is 450 feet tall and has thirty-four floors.

The Grace Church, one of many Catholic churches in Louisiana, has been standing since 1860.

CULTURAL GROUPS

At the time of the Louisiana Purchase, Louisiana's culture was far more French than American. The first white settlers in the area had come from France and French Canada, joined later by Spanish traders. The descendants of these early settlers were known as Creoles, a term which originally meant "native of the colony." Today, the word means different things to different people. It can refer to a variety of combinations of French, Spanish, African, and Caribbean cultures.

QUICK FACTS

Famous creole cuisine includes gumbo and pralines, a tasty dessert.

Creoles speak a form of French, Spanish, or Portuguese.

Some people of Creole ancestry still practice their traditional way of life.

Cajun dancing mixes tradition, a closeness of family, and a zest for life.

Louisiana is the only state with a large population of Cajuns. Cajuns are descendants of the Acadians, who were driven out of Canada in the 1700s. They would not pledge **allegiance** to the King of England.

The term "Cajun" comes from the French-Canadian word "Acadian," and it refers to a group of people and their culture that are only found in Louisiana.

The Cajuns are another important cultural group. In 1755, British soldiers drove 15,000 French colonists from the eastern part of Canada now known as Nova Scotia. These settlers had named that land Acadia. After leaving their home and setting off on a long search for a new one, about 4,000 Acadians arrived in Louisiana. They brought their French culture with them. Today, descendants of these people are known as Cajuns. Many of these people are still French speaking, even though they have blended with Haitian, Spanish, English, German, and Native American cultures to form the modern Cajun culture.

Another name for an accordion is a "squeeze box." It is pulled in and out to produce sound.

ARTS AND ENTERTAINMENT

More than almost anything else, Louisiana is known for Mardi Gras. It is a festival brought to Louisiana by the French. Its name means "Fat Tuesday" in French. It comes from the day when people would slay the fattened calf before Lent and have a feast.

Today, Mardi Gras season begins with a series of parties across the state in January. However, it is New Orleans that has the biggest Mardi Gras of all. For nearly two months every year, the city is alive with music, dancing, colorful street parades, costumes, and floats. More than 1 million visitors enjoy the wild celebration.

QUICK FACTS

New Orleans is often called "The Big Easy" because of its easy-going lifestyle.

The first opera performance in America was held in Louisiana in 1796.

The Louisiana State Museum is the state's oldest and biggest museum. Its displays are spread out over several buildings.

During Mardi Gras parades, beads, coins, balls, cups, and trinkets are thrown into the crowd.

Jazz has been called the "rhythm of human life."

Among the most famous Louisiana jazz greats are Louis Armstrong, Jelly Roll Morton, the Marsalis family, and most recently, Harry Connick, Jr.

Jazz is often considered to be America's great contribution to music.

In recent years, energetic **zydeco** music has blended with rock, rap, jazz, and soul music.

Although the exact history is not clear, **jazz** was probably first played in New Orleans, moving up the Mississippi River to Memphis, St. Louis, and finally arriving in Chicago. The early New Orleans sound goes back to tribal African drum beats and European classical music. It has also been influenced by blues and gospel music. This helps explain why it is difficult to define jazz. Around 1891, it is said that a New Orleans barber named Buddy Bolded picked up his cornet and blew the first notes of jazz. Since then, the jazz sound has been played by many notable musicians, many of whom came from Louisiana.

A very different form of music found only in Louisiana is the accordion music of the Cajuns. A Cajun band is made up of a fiddle, guitar, push-button accordion, and a set of steel triangles. The tunes are lively and usually sung in French. Almost every song is fast-paced and written with dancing in mind.

Zydeco is a newer style of music, growing out of the Creole tradition called "La La." It also uses the push-button accordion, as well as a **rub-board** and spoons.

A rub-board is a washboard that is slung over the shoulders and played with a spoon.

SPORTS

The New Orleans Saints of the National Football League is the only team Louisiana has in the four major professional sports. With no teams in Major League Baseball, the National Basketball Association, or the National Hockey League, Louisianians focus a lot of their sporting attention on football.

Although the Saints have never won the Super Bowl, they play in the stadium that has hosted more Super Bowls than any other. The Superdome has been home to five Super Bowls: in 1978, 1981, 1986, 1990, and 1997. It is because of this claim to fame that New Orleans is often called Super Bowl City by sports fans.

QUICK FACTS

The Superdome is the world's largest indoor stadium and is used for a lot more than football. The stadium still holds the record for the world's largest indoor concert, with the Rolling Stones drawing 87,500 screaming fans in 1981.

When the Superdome opened in 1975, it was promoted as "a triumph of [human] imagination." It is so large, Houston's impressive Astrodome would fit inside it.

The New Orleans Saints often play in their hometown stadium, the Superdome. The Superdome is a super size, with 166,000 square feet of exhibit space.

QUICK FACTS

The longest boxing match in history was held in New Orleans in April 1893. It lasted 110 rounds, which took seven hours and nineteen minutes to fight. The match ended in a tie.

The Sugar Bowl is held every year on or around New Year's Day.

To increase excitement and create fan loyalty, the New Orleans Saints returned to Thibodaux for their 2000 training camp. They ended their eleven-year stint training in Wisconsin to return to stifling 90° F weather and enormous mosquitos!

Another major football event that takes place in the Superdome is the annual Sugar Bowl, in which a challenging team takes on the leading college team in the Southeastern Conference.

Football at the college level has long been an important part of Louisiana's sporting life. The Fighting Tigers of Louisiana State University have been competing for more than 60 years, and another well-known football team is found at Grambling State University in northern Louisiana.

Louisiana is a big football state. It supports its professional and university teams. The Sugar Bowl football game draws thousands of people each year.

Brain Teasers

1

Where in Louisiana is Super Bowl City?

Answer: New Orleans

2

When was Louisiana purchased from Napoleon?

Answer: It was bought in 1803.

3

What does Tabasco Sauce have to do with Louisiana?

Answer: The sauce was first made from tabasco peppers on the state's Avery Island.

4

Who were the Cajun people before they started calling themselves Cajuns?

Answer: They were French Canadians who did not want to stay in Acadia once the English took control.

5

Why is there a pelican on the flag of Louisiana?

Answer: It is the official state bird.

7

These three Louisiana explorers are known by other names. What are they?

a) René-Robert Cavelier
b) Pierre Le Moyne
c) Jean Baptiste Le Moyne

Answer:
a) La Salle
b) Iberville
c) Bienville

6

What is the most important product in Louisiana's fishing industry?

Answer: While crayfish are important, shrimp are the most important. The annual shrimp catch is worth $300 million.

8

What am I?

My name means "Fat Tuesday" in French.

I am the most famous festival in the United States. Most people think of me as a party that lasts for several months. I take place in New Orleans, Louisiana, every year.

Answer: Mardi Gras

FOR MORE INFORMATION

Books

Kent, Deborah. *America the Beautiful: Louisiana*. Children's Press, 1988.

Aylesworth, Thomas G. *Let's Discover the States: South Central*. Chelsea House Publishers, 1988.

World Almanac and Book of Facts. Primedia Reference, 1999

Web sites

There are many great web sites on Louisiana on the Internet. Here are a few you can look at to find out more about this beautiful state:

Tour Louisiana
www.louisianatravel.com

General Louisiana Information Site
www. state.la.us/state/student.htm

Louisiana Department of Culture, Recreation, and Tourism
www.crt-state.la.us

General Louisiana Information page
www.50states.com/louisiana.htm

Some web sites stay current longer than others. To find more Louisiana web sites, use your Internet search engines to look up such topics as "Louisiana," "Mardi Gras," "zydeco," or any other topic you want to research.

GLOSSARY

allegiance: loyalty or obedience to a country, ruler, or cause

bayous: marshy offshoots of a river

gumbo: a type of soup or stew thickened by adding okra, which is a vegetable. It also refers to the mixed African-American and Creole culture in Louisiana.

immunity: being able to fight off disease

indigo: a plant that is used to make blue dye

jambalaya: a spicy Cajun dish

jazz: music and dance that started in Louisiana, with strong African American origins. It is often made up as the musician goes along.

Jesuit: a member of the Roman Catholic religious order

levees: either natural or human-made embankments built up beside a river to prevent flooding

Mardi Gras: means "Fat Tuesday" in French. It is a festival beginning on the final Tuesday before Lent.

parishes: districts originally formed by a church and its leaders. They have become political districts in Louisiana.

port: a harbor where ships dock

rub-board: a rippled board of metal on which people rubbed and washed clothes

sulphur: a nonmetallic element

vital: very important, essential

voodoo: religious beliefs with roots in the West Indies and Africa

zydeco: a type of music with Cajun origins, played largely with fiddles, accordions, rub-boards, and spoons

INDEX